FREDDIE REED'S
ROYAL TOURS
50 Years of Royal Photographs

FREDDIE REED'S
ROYAL TOURS
50 Years of Royal Photographs

DAVID & CHARLES
Newton Abbot   London

DEDICATION

To Katie, my wife, who held the fort at home, and to our sons Michael and David – so often it was 'Hello' and 'Goodbye'. To their wives Caroline and Sally who were unstinting in their continual help and love, and to our lovely grandchildren Daniel, Tamara and Nicholas. All have made my short spells at home very important.

British Library Cataloguing in Publication Data
Reed, Freddie
   Freddie Reed's royal tours: fifty years of
   royal photographs.
   1. Travel by British royal families, history
   I. Title
   910'.880621

   ISBN 0-7153-9389-8

First published 1989

Typeset by ABM Typographics Ltd, Hull
and printed in Great Britain
by Redwood Burn, Trowbridge
for David & Charles Publishers plc
Brunel House   Newton Abbot   Devon

(Frontispiece): *The Queen Mother responds to the shouts of well-wishers gathered outside Clarence House in London on her birthday in 1970. Hundreds had been waiting, a guards band had played 'Happy Birthday' and as ever nobody went away disappointed. A copy of this picture is on exhibition at Glamis Castle, Scotland.*

CONTENTS

ACKNOWLEDGEMENTS

My grateful thanks go to the *Daily Mirror* for permission to use their pictures, to my colleagues up and down London's Fleet Street, and to the photographic printers who so often produced masterpieces from difficult negatives. I should also like to thank Beryl and the late Reg Hewitt, Mick and Joy Lester, and Irene and Harry Cannon, my truly great friends who accepted with so much grace the many dates that I broke at the last moment and who were so warm on my return.

1
PASSPORT TO A PICTURE WORLD

I n 1930, when I was sixteen years old, the purchase of a second-hand plate camera, for the sum of 12s 6d to be repaid by instalments, gave my messenger boy colleagues on a national daily paper plenty to comment about. Undeterred by their taunts, I incurred further debt by enrolling at a night photographic school, so that my normal working day lasted fifteen hours. Working a six-day week of forty-eight hours or more, at everyone's beck and call in the newspaper office, there was little time for enjoyment. The first two years of my working life at the *Daily Mirror* as a messenger, or tea, boy were very hard. On a salary of £1 a week, I first paid my mother, and the remainder went on fares, food and clothes. Promotion came when William Ryder-Ryder, the Picture Editor, asked me to join him as a junior assistant to work as a courier to the paper's team of photographers. It was an unwritten law never to refuse any task and never to be late with one's copy.

My first photographs were developed underneath our dining-room table, draped with a large cover, in a room with the blinds drawn across the windows. The dim red safelight, lit by oil, made it difficult to breathe, but the system worked. As an inexperienced freelance photographer, continually pestering art editors with items which filled either a half or single column, I purchased a new camera on hire purchase.

Press photographers were not held in high esteem, whatever their status. Invariably, they would carry a huge bag, inside which was a large camera that used sensitised glass plates. Film speeds were low, but quality high, even though the work had to be done in a rush, processing taking less than ten minutes from the start to the delivery of the finished print on the editor's desk. The source of indoor lighting at that time was either magnesium ribbon or flash-powder, both of which were extremely dangerous. The powder was inflammable, while the magnesium ribbon, when alight, dripped like molten lead. A

PASSPORT TO
A PICTURE WORLD

tripod was invariably strapped to the camera bag, increasing the load of twelve single or six double slides, normally enough to cover four stories.

One of my earliest exciting assignments was to collect the exposed plates from a photographer who had pictured King George V and Queen Mary at a London trade exhibition. At a previously arranged venue, a long line of photographers were in position with their cameras, which were all mounted on tripods. Assisted by an aide, the royal couple were ushered into a position four yards opposite the cameramen. Among the now excited, congested group of photographers, one was to give the important signal for them to uncover their lenses simultaneously. Focusing the lenses had already taken place underneath the photographers' black cloths, and the extra skilled members had set their distances. There was a great deal of hesitation while the photographers prepared their cameras, until eventually all the metal sheaths were drawn from the slides to uncover the plates. At this point, lens caps, or even trilby hats were still shielding the lenses and the photographers were waiting for the signal that they should uncover them. A second later, the leading photographer, with his huge flash pan held high, set it off with a resounding boom, resulting in a giant sheet of flame that rose into the air. It is not surprising that some of the early photographs show people with startled expressions, or even closed eyes, for they knew what to expect. The light was very strong and the subject had to remain very still. Once the flash was over, the whole area was covered with white dust. Then there was the mad rush to Fleet Street to beat the agencies who were in competition to produce the first pictures of an event. Prints were soaked in methylated spirit – a quick-drying process – and distributed in fantastically short times.

I then found myself attending society weddings, famous sports meetings and events attended by members of the royal family. At the old renowned Brooklands race track, Malcolm Campbell, the world-speed breaker who was later knighted, asked me to assist him by taking a few laps ride in his Bentley and pumping oil. (His son Donald died attempting the world water speed record in the Lake District much later. The editor had me escort his wife Tonia Bern to Lake Coniston in the North just after his death.)

When the first portable telephoto machine arrived, Harry Guy Bartholomew decided that I should operate it, although I had no knowledge of photo telegraphy. From then onwards, I was constantly attending new venues and was rarely at home. I learned to travel light – with no luggage in fact – and to live under constant pressure. I was moved to Manchester and, as a result of covering a train crash at

Warrington, Lancashire, my photographs were published for the first time on the front page. The editor lauded my efforts and sent me 10s 6d, out of which I had to pay for the plates and flash-powder.

As the potential of the new telephoto machines began to be realised, I moved to Darlington, from where I was to supply five pictures a day from agents, and from my own camera, for a special edition seven days a week. The machine was wired up to the bottom of my bed. My next move was to Newcastle-upon-Tyne where I covered every type of news event over a wide area – disasters, ship launches, ships aground, visits by diplomats and royalty, the launching of the *Queen Mary* and giant battleships, flying with the RAF and romances of every kind.

During the early 1940s, King George and Queen Elizabeth were touring the shipyards along the Tyne. It was raining heavily, making movement unpleasant not only for the royal couple, but for everyone else as well. The king personally thanked everyone for their efforts. With water cascading off our cameras, taking photographs was almost impossible and the second day saw no change in the weather. During her visit, the queen noticed three young lads on her route and went over and spoke to them personally. While I struggled in the rain to photograph the group, the queen waited while I removed the white hot flash-bulb, and I was able to take a second shot. Before she moved away, the queen asked if I had got the picture I wanted. As the tour ended, the king and queen moved from the waiting limousine to talk to us and thank us for our efforts.

I was appointed Northern Art Editor in Manchester, then, before the year was out, to Art Editor, then Picture Editor, of the *Daily Mirror* in London, my base for the last years of the war. Having been used to covering events as they happened, a desk job had its frustrations for me, particularly as I had to direct a first-class team of photographers to assignments across the world. Every day, without exception, the paper has to go to press at a certain time and it must contain as much interesting material as possible. Being photo-journalist or desk executive has never been a job for the faint hearted. Having experience of both, I know the pain of seeing photographs being discarded like waste paper by editors, and I also understand how difficult it is to get the shot that matters every time.

PASSPORT TO
A PICTURE WORLD

2
A ROYAL
SHADOW

Royal tours were originally the privileged domain of a few selected reporters and photographers, the cost of which was shared among the Fleet Street and provincial newspapers. The intense competition of getting pictures back to England fast, while the newspapermen were caught in a whirlwind of activity in another part of the world increased enormously. The results of the coverage of my first royal tour were a success, thus helping to boost sales, so it was a matter of course that I should be sent to cover the next tour by a member of the royal family. With me went ex-Roedean schoolgirl Anne Lloyd-Williams, daughter of a police chief, an ambitious and hard-working journalist. But between our attendance at royal events, we were constantly travelling to cover news items worldwide, whether they were disasters, wars, the Olympics, sports or features of general interest.

My shadowing of the royal family during their official duties extended over thirty-five years so that eventually the picture files of the *Daily Mirror* were crammed with records of royal tours and state visits abroad, from places as far apart as the Arctic to tropical Africa, the remote corners of South America to the middle of Australia. My cases had to be large and strong to carry sufficient plates, films, developers and cameras to last as long as three months without returning home.

Having seen the Queen and Prince Philip together on so many official visits and having spent as many as fifteen or sixteen hours a day following them on one of their tours, it is obvious that they are immensely popular. The Queen herself is probably the most photographed person in the world and I have exposed plates and film on her about 200,000 times over the years. She has succeeded in combining forty years of marriage and family life with one of the most exacting jobs in the world.

Although royal tours appear glamorous, attended as they are by huge gatherings in interesting places, the timetable of events can be extremely exacting and tiring. The day's schedule is worked out on a minute-to-minute basis of the royal couple's every move from early morning until their departure for bed. The doctor who accompanies the royal family on tour has the difficult task of ensuring that they are well enough to attend the events that have been prepared for them, for the preparations will indeed have been costly and involve many people.

Photographers who cover royal events must be prepared to be jostled by crowds, while they are loaded down to the point where their backs are breaking with the weight of their camera equipment and they may be restricted by petty, over-zealous officialdom. And in the tropics, they may be suffering from the local stomach bug while perspiring profusely in their suits under the heat of the sun. But press photographers would not change places with any one of their colleagues in the office. Patience is essential on royal tours – long hours may be spent standing hemmed into a tight corner – and endurance and fitness are vital. Time seems to be of no importance and mealtimes pass without food or drink being taken. Although exhaustion often takes over and the photographer wonders why he is earning a living this way, covering royal events and having the satisfaction of seeing his photographs published for thousands of readers to enjoy makes him feel in a privileged position.

Members of the royal family are able to appreciate the technical problems involved in photography for, with the exception of Prince Charles, they are all good photographers and they have often helped in setting up a photograph – for which I have been grateful. Prince Philip is well known for his wildlife photographs, Princess Anne knows how to wield a long focus lens with expertise and the Queen herself has always used a 35mm camera which has stood the test of time.

Even though the Queen has so little free time, she somehow finds time to do those intimate things which show a deep regard and feeling for people. When my colleague reporter, the late Anne Lloyd-Williams, was taken ill and collapsed in Adelaide, Australia, we rushed home from Perth and she was hospitalised in London. After Anne's death a short time later, a hospital official told me that the Queen had requested that a personal report of Anne's condition should be sent to her daily. On another occasion, photographer Reginald Davis was near to collapse in the heat of the noonday sun during a civic ceremony in Suva, Fiji. Although we were not near the dais on which the royal party was sitting, Reginald's condition was obviously noticed for, next day when we were in New Zealand, the Queen stopped the processional car and inquired after his health. I experienced another

A ROYAL SHADOW

A ROYAL SHADOW

example of the Queen's genuine concern for people when I was covering a tour in Bonn, Germany. As the streets were very crowded I had climbed onto a high wall for a vantage point. When the royal car approached my camera sight, I was pushed and fell about ten feet out of view. At a reception the next day, the Queen asked me where I had vanished and whether I had been hurt.

Having travelled some miles in the Queen's personal limousine during a royal drive, I know from personal experience what problems arise during a cavalcade, particularly in a foreign country. On the occasion of a very successful tour of Portugal, when the people came to within a few feet of the vehicle, I had no doubt regarding the necessity for security when the royal family is on the move. Crowds lined the streets throughout their tour and tons of flower blossoms and mimosa were spread across the roads along their journey. Eventually, the royal couple arrived in Oporto, from where they were to fly to London. Here the crowds were astonishing. Press photographers had the privilege of following the royal car in an open-top motor coach, giving us an elevated view of the scenes. The pressure of the enormous crowds prevented many of the local people from getting a view of the Queen, who was obviously aware of the disappointment of many onlookers. Sir Richard Colville, her Press Secretary, then approached Eddie Worth of Associated Press and myself and asked if the Queen could change places with us. In return, we were offered her car. The royal standard was flying from the bonnet as we clambered into the luxurious limousine.

Seated high on the back seat in the coach, the royal couple had an uninterrupted view, as did the Portuguese people. However, some people stared into the limousine and caught sight of Eddie and myself. We lowered the electrically operated windows only a few times as the crowds surged to within a few feet of us, because as we did so the car was immediately showered with flowers and rice. Every time that the windows were lowered more rose petals, mimosa and rice were flung at our faces and landed in our laps. The royal visit had been a great success and our story was published on the front page of the London dailies and broadcast on the radio.

One of my strangest assignments was the result of a tip that was to send reporter Howard Johnson and myself to Malta. Prince Philip was attending the independence ceremony on the island and an informer had it on great authority that the Queen would arrive quietly in Malta, one of her favourite places because of its association with Prince Philip when he was serving with the Navy. The Queen's visit was to be completely incognito and unannounced. It was believed that she would watch the ceremony unseen and, after paying tribute at the war memorial, she would fly home again. I spent an entire twenty-four hours with a camera hidden under my coat from the time of our arrival on Malta. As I was unable to leave the area of the war memorial, Johnnie brought me sandwiches and coffee every few hours. I had to observe every solitary figure who passed, for I had no idea how the Queen would be dressed, nor indeed what disguise she might be wearing. However, at the end of the celebrations, our attempts to witness the Queen incognito – if indeed she had ever arrived – were a total failure.

In 1963 the Queen and Prince Philip arrived in Chicago and were received with a ticker-tape welcome. We had arrived just a little earlier and had had no time to take up a good position for photography – even though the *Mirror* was on strike we still had to send pictures back every day. At the Hilton Hotel later that evening I received a cable instructing us to return to London as the pictures would not be used owing to the strike. I flew home shortly afterwards, in time to hear the announcement from Buckingham Palace that the Queen was pregnant (Prince Edward was born in 1964).

A ROYAL SHADOW

3
WELL-LAID PLANS

The forward planning of a royal tour for a photographer on a daily newspaper starts some weeks or months earlier. This not only entails organising planes, boats, cars, radio links, darkrooms, locations of radio stations and vital airport distances from cities, but also the minute-to-minute timing to and from actual venues. Visas have to be arranged, it is necessary to check with each country that they will allow the export of undeveloped film and customs sheets must be obtained to ensure that the cameras can not only be taken into the countries to be visited but also taken out again. A plentiful supply of films must be taken to cover a trip that may last as long as twelve weeks. Developers, printing paper and fixing chemicals are also taken, as the photographer never knows if he can guarantee having his films printed while on tour.

As much as possible has to be arranged before the press group leaves London. Vitally important is the knowledge of any schedules that will cover personal travel ahead of the royal party and the daily supply of pictures being sent to London. It is therefore necessary to know the fastest way from one place to another by any mode of transport, for photographs must be sent to the editor as soon as possible. World transport timetables are studied in advance, for without them it is useless even to start a long tour. One also has to take into account religious festivals which occur at irregular dates in different countries, when few planes may depart.

Whenever members of the royal family are on tour abroad, particularly on official visits, the localities are generally *en fête*. This also means that hotels are booked up well in advance by visiting dignitaries, thus making accommodation in short supply. A sudden influx of people into a town can make even a single room difficult to find. Arranging a room in a small bush town in the heart of Africa, the USA or even Australia prior to arrival can be a waste of time. In Ethiopia, I spent one night in a noisy, dirty, smelly room above a brothel, alive with pests, and in Hamburg I slept above a fruit shop. From one extreme to another, I have had the President's Suite in a plush Acapulco hotel with a swimming pool on the balcony, a film-star's rooms in Tucson, Arizona, and a suite at the Beverly Hilton, Los Angeles, but have also slept under canvas on safari in Africa. I have slept on the back of a lorry, many times in airports and railway stations, at the Waldorf Astoria in New York, and at many Hilton hotels. Meals can only be taken late at night when the royalty are beyond the camera's range.

The royal party normally arrives at its destination exactly on time. As soon as the plane or car door opens, or their ship or launch pulls alongside the quay, the local band breaks into rhythm, actually timing the music to start the British national anthem in Britain or the local anthem as the royal visitors touch foreign soil. From the moment of their arrival, they meet dignitaries, VIPs, small children, Scouts, Brownies, the Red Cross, a guard-of-honour, and so on. Photo-graphers are normally two hours ahead of the official party, and they must keep up with all the day's events without respite.

Before long, in my career, I was covering events at Windsor and Holyrood, the White House and the Kremlin, in the palaces of Holland, Chiang Mai in Thailand, India, Ethiopia, Denmark, Norway and Sweden, the Peacock Throne Room in Tehran and, of course, Buckingham Palace. Wherever I went, it was important to follow the protocol and customs of the hosts to the letter. The pageantry and ceremonies meant so much to the people involved.

In some countries, the scenes were inspiring, having taken months to prepare. In nearly every town or city schools would have a few days' holiday to join in the celebrations. On occasions, the enthusiasm which followed a royal visit could, and sometimes did, lead to near disaster when the guards could not contain the number of people lining the streets.

Although crowd situations are generally under control, I have witnessed several frightening moments, such as one occasion in Valparaiso, Chile. It was a warm day and everything was going very smoothly until the lined route of servicemen diminished. The crowd moved in closer and closer towards the Queen until they were only a few feet away, growing in numbers rapidly as others rushed to join them. Within seconds, the Queen could not be seen. My camera was torn from my neck as the excitement rose. Men and women with children so small they could not see daylight, were thrust into a compression of bodies. It was frightening to be lifted completely off-balance and carried in a sea of humanity without any control and being almost crushed when the two armies of well-wishers met in the

WELL-LAID PLANS

15

WELL-LAID PLANS

middle of the road. The situation was alarming for a few moments before the royal party's escorts entered the fray and forcibly cleared a path.

The Queen and other members of the royal family are well aware of the need for publicity on tours wherever they may be, and their enthusiasm to help has been one of the primary aids to our coverage, although it is seldom appreciated by some of the media. When the Queen was due to visit Ghana during the reign of President Nkruma, it was suggested that she should postpone her trip because the president's statue in Accra had been attacked with bombs. Sir Winston Churchill had tried to persuade the Queen against the visit, but she continued the tour as arranged with remarkable success.

A few hours after landing, a reception was held at Christiansborg Castle for the international press. I was a few minutes late because I had covered the Queen's arrival in Accra for the rest of the press, as it was my turn on the rota. I then had to process the film and dash to the radio station, where I received the dismal news that sunspots and severe interference made it impossible for reception in London. The luxury surroundings of the castle and the drinks on offer from silver trays did not synchronise with my feelings, and while I was talking to a colleague from the local *Daily Graphic*, for whom I was also supplying pictures, I turned round and found myself facing the Queen. Her charming greeting of 'The old team again – how long have you been here?' addressed to Anne Lloyd-Williams, my reporter colleague from the *Daily Mirror*, and myself delighted us because she had obviously remembered our conversation of an earlier royal tour in which we had said that we spent more time together following her and other members of the royal family, than we spent at home.

A little later she asked how the arrangements were going. In the strictest belief that the truth should not be avoided because somehow the information always got through anyway, I replied that no pictures would appear in the London dailies next day and explained why. The Queen immediately replied that she had just been speaking to an official from the radio station and had been told that everything was working well. She summoned a secretary and not long afterwards a picture arrived in London.

In the early days we had to rely on the Cable and Wireless Company to get pictures and copy to London, and their stations were based only in cities, generally with only one picture machine. It was a case of first come, first served. Often the pictures appeared with the credit line 'Picture by Radio' or 'Picture by Wire' which was some excuse for the poor quality. It was in Accra, Ghana, that Terry Fincher and I stripped to our pants to process films in a bedroom. We made two hurried prints, and then ran at top speed – in competition with the Associated Press photographer – down the street to the cable head.

Royal tours abroad would draw vast crowds eager to see a real queen. At Kaduna, Nigeria, for example, thousands of men, women and children gathered from all over the country, some taking days, even weeks of travel to attend. The chiefs brought their entire entourages, who carried all their possessions, each item being carried on top of the head. The chiefs themselves were also carried. Horsemen decorated their saddles with jewels and braids and wore gold spurs, while others carried and played musical instruments of all shapes and sizes. The giant procession continued until midday, until the finale, when the horsemen galloped past the royal stand in a tremendous cloud of dust that enveloped everybody. People returned contented that they had seen a real Queen.

The Queen then had to attend a state luncheon, followed by a reception, and a banquet at night. At that event, the people sang their own lyrics to the British anthem to greet the royal visitor. They sang 'Nigeria, Nigeria, the land we love so well . . .' finishing with the words 'The land of Mrs Queen . . .' They ended with a great cheer – and their sincerity was unmistakable.

Following the royal family into the heat of Africa or to the cold of the Arctic has its problems for the photographer, but being something of a photographer herself, the Queen, like Princess Anne and Prince Philip, understands those problems. I had the opportunity to use the Queen's camera when she wanted a picture for her own album. Using her 35mm camera, I photographed the Queen leaving an igloo in the Arctic. Naturally, I would have liked to have sent the photographs back to my editor, but the picture is kept safely in the Queen's own album.

At a reception in Buckingham Palace I was the only cameraman to photograph a group of Commonwealth ministers with the Queen. It was a large gathering and, spread shoulder to shoulder, very wide. The Queen was in the middle, but I could not move back any further to get them all in the frame. The Queen herself, however, stepped out of the group to help me. She addressed the group and asked them to edge in a little at the sides and, eventually, when this had been accomplished, she turned and asked me if that was an improvement. She knew, of course, that it was, thanked the ministers, and then walked back to her own place and gave me a huge smile.

A large gathering of the royal families from all over the world was assembled in the Dam Palace, Amsterdam, to be photographed for posterity on the occasion of Queen Juliana's and Prince Bernhardt's

WELL-LAID PLANS

twenty-fifth wedding anniversary. The official photographer had a large camera on a tripod and, when he had set up the shot, asked everybody to be still. I was taken aback when I heard him say 'Watch the birdie' and the huge group of royalty stared in amazement as the photographer uncovered a toy whistling bird attached to the top of his camera. The result of this amusing incident produced a smile from everybody and a good picture.

During that same trip I was in the Throne Room of the Dam Palace for an evening reception. To get the photograph I required, I hid in the giant fireplace behind some potted plants. As the Queen moved into position a few yards away, I appeared and took the shot. She was very surprised, smiled and looked amused as I hid myself again among the greenery. The incident proved the importance of being in the right position at the right time.

There are occasions when it is essential for photographers and cameramen to remain hidden from view – for example, at religious ceremonies and royal weddings, or the opening of parliament, and so on.

During the Queen's Silver Jubilee ceremony at St Paul's in 1977, I was some feet above her at an oblique angle and about seven yards away from where she was sitting with Prince Philip. Hidden from view with long lenses protruding through the metal framework of temporary tubular scaffolding, we were shielded by draped material. We climbed into position a long time before the guests were due to arrive and stayed there until the ceremony was over.

There are occasions when photographers happen to be in position at the precise moment that an unplanned incident has created a good picture. For instance, on a very windy day in Wellington, New Zealand, in 1963 when strong gusts of wind were playing havoc with bunting and flags and, of course, with hats, coats and dresses, the Queen and Prince Philip arrived to tour the city. Moving a few feet from the limousine on arrival at the function, the updraught of the wind caught the hem of the Queen's skirt – a problem the royal dressmakers had anticipated for the Queen's hems are weighted. Fighting to keep the dress down, the Queen's face broke into a huge smile. She moved forward, holding her dress down with both hands. The smile continued on her face until she was well inside the building, having handled the incident with elegant amusement. The photographs of the incident were published in England.

Occasionally, when things go wrong and someone breaks the security barrier, the ever-vigilant Prince Philip is always ready to protect the Queen. In Penang the tremendous crowd had surged forward during the Queen's walkabout. Suddenly a peak-capped man rushed forward and tried to place a garland of flowers over her head. Prince Philip steered the man's hand firmly, but gently away, placing his hand on the intruder's shoulder and holding him at a distance, while offering a kind word. A moment which could have been dangerous had passed, without incident.

The late King Frederick of Denmark, a charming monarch who always had a warm and friendly greeting, was still able to smile as he awaited the arrival of the Queen and Prince Philip in Copenhagen, even though he was in pain. The wind was blowing hard, it was very cold, and he was in uniform, when he walked towards me with a limp. We talked about the weather, then he explained: 'I've got lumbago – a fine old time to get such a complaint, with Her Majesty due to arrive at any minute.' With his hand on his back, he went forward to greet the Queen, helping her into an open landau. His first act was to call for a fur wrap for the Queen's shoulders so that she would be warm enough for her drive through the city.

The Queen is always aware of things that don't go to plan and she takes the mishaps in her stride. She is a very human and warm-hearted person, fully aware that everybody at some time or other experiences those fearful moments when things go wrong.

When you travel on exceptionally detailed programmes, you can never predict how far your well-laid plans will go astray. In 1970 I was accompanying the Queen, Prince Philip, Prince Charles and Princess Anne on a tour of the North West Territories of Canada immediately after working in Washington. Normally, I would have had my cameras serviced to rid them of the grease which tends to slow down the shutter in very cold weather. However, I had been advised that the temperature wouldn't drop below 50°F. Unfortunately, the information was incorrect, because there was plenty of ice and we were not suitably dressed to keep warm – hardly the ideal conditions for taking photographs.

One of the highlights of the tour was to be the viewing of the midnight sun from a place named Tuktoyaktuk on the Beaufort Sea. Great interest developed with all the possibilities of seeing this wonderful sight, and we followed the royal flight from the town of Aklavik. While the lighter aircraft carrying the royal party stayed on top of the packed ice-strip, our giant Hercules, with over a hundred press people aboard, sank a wheel through the melting surface. Howling huskies in teams – still reined to sledges outside their wooden homes – greeted us as we moved into the town, while the weather worsened. At the bewitching hour of midnight, when all were to view the glory of the midnight sun, the royal party arrived at the chosen viewpoint on time in a freezing high wind, swept by ice cold

WELL-LAID PLANS

rain. They stood looking out to sea at low cloud and little else, hoping for the rare sight of the midnight sun, but even though each was wearing a hooded parka, the weather was becoming distinctly uncomfortable minute by minute. The exercise had proved fruitless. By this time, any chance of anyone – apart from the royal party – getting away was hopeless. The light aircraft bearing the royal family managed an easy take-off in the high wind, while the press were shepherded to the assembly hall of the local school.

It had been a long day and night for the Queen and other members of the royal party, which had simply ended in disappointment. They had all started out from Frobisher Bay at 10 o'clock in the morning, heading for Resolute, 850 miles away, from where the Queen and Princess Anne continued to Aklavik. Prince Philip and Prince Charles took off for Hoodoo, on the ice, a few hundred miles further north in a Hercules aircraft. Then the royal family were reunited for the viewing of the midnight sun. By the time they settled down in the early hours of the following morning, at the end of a nineteen-hour day, the Queen and Princess Anne had flown about 2,000 miles and Prince Philip and Prince Charles about 2,900 miles. Bernard Hesketh and myself travelled to Aklavik in very bad weather, telephoned the copy to Fleet Street, and despatched the film on a jet heading for London. When the pictures arrived, however, they were over-exposed and the picture editor rejected them.

A few weeks later when we were back in London, Picture Editor Len Greener asked if a good photograph was available to illustrate Princess Anne's birthday. I did indeed have a shot of the princess and Prince Charles laughing. A full page of this photograph appeared in the *Daily Mirror* and later won the award of the Royal Picture of the Year. By sheer coincidence, it was Princess Anne herself who presented the prize at a London hotel. She said, 'If I may pick out one of the winners, a familiar face to me is Freddie Reed, who has been taking royal pictures for longer than I can remember. He has been around professionally twice as long as I have.'

The progress of photographic equipment, with the use of high speed flashes and fast film has made the life of an international cameraman a great deal easier. One of my best pictures of the Queen was taken in Malta in 1954. Using a 9 x 12cm plate camera called a VN with a giant 45 flash-bulb linked to a compur shutter, the light source was powerful. In darkness, the cameras had to be pre-set to what the photographer thought would be the right focal distance from the spot where the subject was standing – not an easy task.

In Valletta, Malta, I was waiting at the landing stage for the arrival of the Queen from *Britannia* to attend a civic banquet. She stepped off the blue and gold boat in the dark, where I waited with my finger on the shutter, until she had both feet planted firmly on the quay. The blinding flash a few seconds later flooded the area and I just caught a glimpse of a figure in a tiara. I despatched the film of my day's work on the night plane to London without knowing what the results would be. Next morning, to my surprise, the editor telephoned me with congratulations for such wonderful shot of the Queen, looking, he said, very elegant in a naval boat cloak. I saw the photograph for the first time on the front page of the paper the following day.

During this visit, the late Lord Louis Mountbatten was at the centre of one of the rarest fleet reviews and naval displays, which he saw from the bridge of HMS *Glasgow*. It was planned that lines of warships of all types and sizes should criss-cross at speed off the island. The talk in the officers' mess was that the event would be a fiasco. Sitting beside the commanding officer in the leading flight of Shackleton aircraft, which flew over the *Glasgow* at the critical moment, the sight was one which will never be re-enacted. The sea was filled with naval vessels all sailing at speed, performing a manoeuvre that looked as if they were heading for each other. The three Shackleton aircraft homing in on this galaxy of activity were wing-tip to wing-tip when the order from Lord Louis 'Come in like a flight of aircraft, not a gaggle of geese' filled our ears. Flying lower and lower, we headed straight over the bridge of the battleship and received the words loud and clear from Lord Louis 'Fine show chaps' as the planes headed down the line to peel off a few miles later. It is not being just sentimental to say that the sight of the fleet review in the Mediterranean was a marvel to me.

When I was having a chat with Sir William Heseltine, then Press Secretary, now Private Secretary, to the Queen, the topic of the Queen's birthday pictures arose. He told me that I was to be honoured with an invitation to photograph the Queen in the grounds of Frogmore, Windsor. I was to be accompanied by one photographer from an agency, together with the late Ronnie Read of television and a newsreel representative. The result of the photography session was a set of delightful pictures of the royal family: the Queen, Prince Philip, Prince Charles, Princess Anne, Prince Andrew and the baby Prince Edward being pushed in his pram with the help of his older brother. Between times, Prince Andrew was enjoying sliding down the grassy bank among the daffodils where he picked a flower for his mother. Meanwhile, Princess Anne placed a daffodil on Prince Edward's head while he was being carried by the Queen. All the opposition papers gave my photographs large bylines – a rare accolade – and commented on the informality of the pictures.

WELL-LAID PLANS

WELL-LAID PLANS

One of the most exciting journeys I have ever made was on the royal yacht *Britannia* with the Queen, Prince Philip, President Eisenhower, Vice-President Nixon and Canadian Prime Minister Diefenbaker, on the occasion of the grand opening of the St Lawrence Seaway in 1959. Crowds cheered, cannons fired, streamers littered the sky and planes roared overhead when the yacht broke the giant tapes. Everywhere the crowds packed the locks and there were multi-coloured decorations on both banks. On one of those warm days which I would have loved to go on forever, a happy sound was created by bands, radios and people singing, but the pictures had to be sent back to England. I had to leave the yacht by means of a tall ladder when the vessel went through a lock.

It was in Canada, too, that the Queen's whistle-stop train journey was something of an Olympic course for the accompanying photographers and reporters. As the train approached a station, we had to leap off just before it came to a final stop. From there it was a dash down the track alongside the coaches to the rear, where, by excellent judgement, the end of the last carriage coincided with a red carpet where the Queen was already waiting to alight.

The Queen was greeted by a reception committee and was then driven around the town, stopping at certain places, and then finally headed back to the waiting train. Our carriages were always about four or five down the line. As soon as the Queen arrived, she climbed aboard, and the train continued on to its next destination. With cameras swinging from our necks and having to contend with tightly packed crowds to reboard the train, the tour demanded a great deal of physical energy.

There have been two occasions on which some exceptionally good photographs of mine have been lost in the darkroom. On the first occasion, I had photographed the Swedish royal family on the quayside in Stockholm where they were waiting to board a boat to meet the Queen and Prince Philip a little distance away. When they met, the Queen was deciding what jewellery she should wear. Her jewellery box was offered to her by the young Prince Gustav, who took out a number of pieces and placed them either around her neck or on her dress, replacing and rechoosing certain items. Being the only photographer in attendance, I considered that I was very lucky to shoot this unique scene. The twelve photographs were intended for the *Daily Mirror*, although it was Saturday and we were helping the Sunday edition. On that particular day, however, four photographers who had been working in the darkroom at our base in Stockholm had lost their film in processing. After great deliberation, going over the problems and being assured by the technician that all would be well, I

offered my film to the *Sunday Mirror*. Unfortunately, however, they successfully ruined my film too. I can still see in my imagination those photographs that would have delighted the world.

The second occasion when such a disaster occurred was in Accra, when Princess Marina was touring Ghana. The local paper, the *Daily Graphic*, processed all my film because they themselves were publishing my work. At the end of the morning, the local judges had gathered to meet the princess who was at the top of a flight of steps, at the entrance to the building. One overweight judge, decked in his robes and chain of office, had found the heat rather exhausting and tiring. His wig was askew and his attempt to climb the steps was difficult for him. The princess leaned over from the top of the steps and, with both hands, took his hands and started to pull. The judge's wig became more askew and the princess had to take more leverage to hold him. The faces, the scene and the judge provided a set of pictures that were quite unique. Unfortunately, however, two hours later, the film was ruined in the darkroom when someone accidentally entered through the unlocked door. So the record of those unusual scenes of the princess and the judge's wig are held only in my memory.

What happened to David McNeill of the then *Sunday Pictorial* in Tripoli in 1954 illustrates how good fortune can sometimes favour a photographer covering a royal tour. We had flown in an RAF Shackleton aircraft from Malta to El Adam in Tripoli to meet the Queen who was due to arrive the following day. At dawn, all the pressmen were standing on the air-strip, most of whom were using either a VN or Speed Graphic – both large cameras. Each had a supplementary use of a Rolleiflex for cover. Tension built up among the large group of cameramen from newsreels, television or newspapers as the Queen's aircraft came into view. Just as the Queen's plane touched down, David realised that his camera shutter was jammed. As he reached for his Rolleiflex, the lens fell out of its case and rolled along the tarmac. No one could help him as they were all poised to photograph the Queen as she stepped from the aircraft. In frustration he bent forward and hit his camera on the ground. Within a few seconds the shutter had unjammed and David was able to photograph the Queen along with all the other photographers. An hour later, after the Queen had toured the war graves, an RAF plane took off with photographs that were destined for the London Sunday papers. David's pictures were printed on the front and middle pages.

One of the more exotic royal tours I had covered was when the Queen met the late Emperor Haile Selassie in Ethiopia. Roast sucking pig, together with countless other delicacies, crammed the enormous

WELL-LAID PLANS

tables. Huge log fires blazed out over the priceless carpets, while guests refreshed themselves with the choicest of wines. A day earlier we had been invited to the emperor's palace in Addis Ababa and were met at the gates by two unusual guards – a couple of fully grown lions which were able to move about on long chains. While trying to picture one of them with my super wide angle lens, I didn't realise how near it was and how interested it was in me. It walked straight over to me and knocked me on my back. A few minutes later, photographer Terry Fincher was so startled by it that he leapt over a hedge as fast as an Olympic athlete.

The following day we struggled along the paths of dust to keep up with the royal party that was en route to the Tississat Falls on the Nile. It seemed a long way, but the Queen took it all in her stride. By the time we arrived at the falls, she was enjoying her own exploration of the site. After an official photography session, we returned along the same hot dusty path, and in the evening the Queen had to attend a royal banquet in Addis Ababa.

A year or so later at the palace of the King of Thailand in Chiang Mai, the Queen, Prince Philip and Princess Anne were attending the ceremony in which the group's wrists are tied as an act of friendship. We sat nearby on soft carpets being fed by beautiful girls who were attending the king and Queen Sirikit. Specially rolled cigars, age-old whisky and a display of dancing by the silk-bedecked girls in the light of lanterns, were all to be enjoyed. As a finale, stopping before the king and the lovely Queen Sirikit who were standing with the Queen, Prince Philip and Princess Anne, came many hundreds of girls from the huge grounds, each carrying a candlelit lantern and singing as they passed. It was a glimpse into a fairyland world. Next morning, at dawn, we were off to see elephants working in the lumber camps and doing tricks in their spare time.

4
ON THE ROYAL BAND WAGON

My cameras have been pointing at the royal family for many years, capturing the romances, the delightful moments, the ceremonials and following the progress of the children to adulthood.

The early pictures of Prince Charles and Princess Anne before they started school were always a great attraction to the world at large. When the children were born, the rooftops of buildings around Buckingham Palace were festooned with cameramen from all parts of the globe, aiming giant long focus lenses over the palace grounds to get the earliest picture of the Queen pushing a pram. Between the chimneys photographers spent many days just watching and waiting. One of the most intimate photographs of the royal children at play was taken at St Paul's Bay in Malta in 1954 when the five-year-old Prince Charles and Princess Anne spent a day playing in the rock pools at the seaside followed by a picnic. With them were their much loved uncle and aunt, the late Lord Louis and Lady Edwina Mountbatten.

When Prince Charles went to school in Scotland, journalists and photographers pursued him, and a story emerged of his liking for a sip of liquor. I never witnessed the incident that caused quite a scandal, but I did capture him in the act of toasting his sister, Princess Anne, when they attended the wedding of Lady Pamela Mountbatten to David Hicks at Romsey in 1960 – it was a soft drink.

We followed the prince into every new adventure from school to flying and the Navy, and wherever he went he captured the hearts of people everywhere. When he received his wings during a passing out parade at RAF Cranwell in 1971, there was a proud smile from his father, Prince Philip. In 1976 he was piped aboard when he took command of the minesweeper HMS *Bronington* at the Rosyth Naval Base in Scotland, a post demanding not only qualities of leadership but expert scientific knowledge of the sonar operating equipment on board.

ON THE ROYAL
BAND WAGON

The press followed him to Fiji where he wore garlands of flowers on an official trip. The weather was unpleasant, and on an excursion to watch him fishing, our boat went aground at night. In the early hours and in intense darkness we were taken off a few at a time, in flimsy native canoes, and put down in water that was two feet deep, with nearly a mile to wade ashore in follow-my-leader style, each of us hoping we would not step on a stone fish.

Probably Prince Charles's most difficult trip was to Washington with Princess Anne, during the presidency of Richard Nixon. So many stories had already been invented by journalists of all nations about his meeting with Tricia, the President's daughter. She went with him to a baseball game and explained the rules. She seemed to love every minute of the occasion. Princess Anne stayed a little in the background. Tricia went everywhere with the prince on the very much itemised and planned few days. I had the distinct feeling, standing a few feet away while he said his farewells to the President's wife and Tricia, that he was pleased to be going. His helicopter was only few feet off the lawn of the White House before the American journalists besieged Mrs Nixon and Tricia, asking such questions as 'Are you seeing him again?', and from one of the rather tough Washington ladies, 'Will you be writing each other?' Microphones were aimed at her lips from every conceivable angle.

Prince Charles is very adventurous and will have a go at anything, whatever the risk, or even involve himself in a discussion wherever he happens to be. In 1970, he insisted on joining a gigantic party at 2am on the beach at Yellowknife in the North West Territories of Canada. It was cold and wet as he joined the party until the rain became unbearable.

On safari in the Kenyan bush in 1971, the prince grew a beard because water was at a premium.

In 1971, the prince was due to make a parachute jump, although the Ministry of Defence informed the *Mirror* that the details were a secret. However, my contacts informed me that the jump was to take place at Studland Bay on 28 July. When I arrived, all the car parks were full. The car park attendant, learning who I was, told me to park my car in the already full area, to take a seat and get a cup of tea. He told me that the prince would be the second man out of the second plane. I put up a camera with a 2,000mm lens and waited. I took only two shots, one as the prince left the aircraft, the other as he neared the water.

When we were flying to Nairobi to start a safari in 1971 while Princess Anne did a tour for the Save the Children Fund, the prince asked us to a drinks party as we headed out over the Mediterranean.

From this meeting I learned that his knowledge of world affairs is wide and that he longs to find things out for himself. He has a lively approach, intelligent conversation and enjoys spontaneous good humour, which has made him one of the most popular members of the royal family. There is, however, the more serious side to the life of Prince Charles – the preparation for his role as king. When the Queen officially presented her son to the Welsh people as their future monarch at Caernarvon Castle at the investiture ceremony in July 1969, it was a proud moment when she announced 'Your Prince, my most dear son'. He had been given the title of Prince of Wales in 1958.

Prince Charles's marriage to Lady Diana Spencer was an unforgettable occasion and one of the most delightful days I have ever spent behind a camera.

When Princess Anne was studying French on the continent, I received an 11am telephone call from the editor to be at a venue in the middle of France by 3 o'clock. I dashed to Gatwick, where our waiting Rapide bi-plane had already arranged clearance, and with photographer Tony Eyles, then of *The Sun* (then owned by the Mirror Group), we headed for Nantes. From there we travelled many miles by road, driving as fast as possible. Eventually, we drove into the grounds of a chateau and immediately behind us was the princess with three other girls in a car. We pulled alongside the River Oudon. They alighted from their car, climbed aboard a punt and were away in a few minutes. I quickly took photographs of them and then rushed back to England with the film.

Another frantic trip was made to photograph Princess Anne at Val d'Isère early in the morning when she would be heading for the higher ski slopes. The only way I was able to catch up with her was to fly to Zurich in Switzerland first and then drive south through the night. The weather worsened the further south I drove and the roads were engulfed by walls of snow. However, I reached the princess in time, took a few shots of her and her skiing instructor, and then had to face the return journey back to England by the same route.

In 1971 the Shah of Persia's celebration of the 2,500th anniversary of the founding of the Persian Empire was a memorable event, particularly the pageantry at Persepolis and the delightful site of Shiraz where the Shah had built a town of houses for his guests. Each house was completely covered, just for the occasion, with tent material in traditional colours to represent a royal encampment. The processions and ceremonies continued for several days. When the moment came for the Shah to make his speech at Pasargadae, the original home of the Achaemenian dynasty, where Cyrus the Great lies buried in a tomb, a wind suddenly blew up, slowly at first, then

ON THE ROYAL
BAND WAGON

ON THE ROYAL BAND WAGON

increasing in intensity. It picked up the flags, sent up clouds of sand, gathering momentum every second, and eventually engulfed the podium. It was as if Cyrus himself was gracing the event with his presence. The fierce wind blew right across the scene and then blew itself out, leaving the site as quiet as the desert itself. It was a strange occurrence and people sensed that it was an omen.

I was more than a little apprehensive when I joined the three-day eventers – among them Princess Anne – who were taking part in the European Horse-riding Championships in Kiev, Russia, because I had encountered the difficulties of working in Russia on an earlier trip. When the British horses arrived with their riders in the charter transport, we were already waiting on the airport tarmac. The aircraft was returning straight back to England and I asked the local airport chief if we could send our film to London on the return flight. After much discussion with his officers, they agreed.

The following day, the *Mirror* published our photographs on the front page, although the Russians were not pleased at all because we had not used the official channels to send our films back to England.

On the final day of the Kiev championships, the event finished on Saturday night. Restrictions on the movement of film were to start at midnight and with no planes leaving the country, all the photographers had no answer to the question of how to transport their film out of the country. It was my turn to get the material back to London. That night in my hotel room I filled to the brim a huge sack with television film. At the airport the following day, I was very dubious about the possibility of getting the film through customs. The officers examined every piece of my equipment and checked and rechecked the numbers of the lenses and cameras, but they did not enquire about the sack at my feet, nor did I offer an explanation. My flight out of Russia was a tense one, so I was very relieved when I finally landed in England.

I photographed Princess Anne in 1971 during her tour of Africa for the Save the Children Fund. While she was in Nairobi, she took part in a programme with Valerie Singleton for BBC television. When she visited Treetops in Kenya, she was obviously moved when she read the plaque commemorating the visit of her parents who were staying there when they received the news of the death of George VI.

The princess herself is an adept photographer and can manipulate all the lenses on a 35mm outfit with ease and efficiency. There have, in fact, been occasions when we have stood photographing each other with our long lenses. Not only have I photographed Princess Anne in places as far away as the Arctic and Southeast Asia but on the day of her marriage to Captain Mark Phillips. My last sight of her that day was as she rode down

Buckingham Palace Road in a landau, leaving for their honeymoon.

Princess Alexandra has a delightful personality and she captures the hearts of everybody she meets. She works very hard for handicapped children and the blind and is a successful royal ambassador in her work abroad. After her marriage to the Hon Angus Ogilvy in 1963, I had the honour of photographing their reception in St James's Palace.

During one of her longer tours, into West Africa, our accommodation in some places was primitive to say the least, and we had to work in damp conditions and hindered by millions of flies. We appreciated her concern for our welfare and the efforts that were made to alleviate the bad conditions.

Edward, Duke of Kent, married Miss Katherine Worsley, the daughter of a Yorkshire county family, at York Minster in 1961. It was my task to photograph the bridal procession from a hide just over their heads as they walked to the great door and a waiting crowd. I also photographed other members of the royal family who were waiting to enter the minster prior to the ceremony. In 1962, I photographed their first child, George, Earl of St Andrew's, and in 1964, I attended Windsor Castle to cover the christening of Lady Helen Windsor in the presence of the royal family.

ON THE ROYAL
BAND WAGON

5

THE ROYAL ROSE

Vivacious and glamorous, the young Princess Margaret created new interest for royal tours during the 1950s when she spent several weeks in the West Indies. The Caribbean tour was her first attempt at working to a prolonged minute-to-minute programme. Grenada, Barbados, Antigua, Jamaica – the Caribbean islands greeted the princess enthusiastically. Using large cameras needing glass photographic plates, some of the photographers' undeveloped material had to be sent back to London by plane and was often delayed or lost. David McNeill of the then *Sunday Pictorial* – now the *Sunday Mirror* – lost five weeks' work in transit.

Every evening, the princess's appearance in a new gown caused a great deal of interest and was of vital importance to newspapers. Her grand entrance, however, was so often into a small area hemmed in by photographers, that it was not possible to get a full-length shot. David Johnson and myself therefore placed a flower on the stair where we wished her to stop. She happily co-operated with this idea and we used it on many occasions.

Princess Margaret's tour of the West Indies was such a success that photographers followed her eagerly wherever she went on subsequent trips. Foreign magazines were particularly keen to obtain photographs of her when she was off-duty, relaxing in a bathing suit or bikini, or swimming in the pool – and they were willing to pay a high price for the pictures. The princess had first-hand experience of the pressmen's intrusion when, shortly after her arrival in Vancouver, she looked out of her hotel window to admire the view, to discover that she was looking into the long focus lens of a continental photographer who was positioned on the fire escape, pointing his camera directly into her bedroom. Two days later, a cameraman was lifted by the Mounties from a well-victualled hiding hole near to the princess's bathing spot. He had spent all night there, just waiting.

When he was discovered he was asked to hand in his accreditation. Offers then went out to anybody who might have a picture of the princess in a bikini – money was no object.

I made my first attempt at photographing a rodeo at Williams Lake in British Columbia. The bucking broncos and steers were lined up to come out of the shutes just below the platform of the royal party. We were standing just seven yards away, and a little oblique from the gate. The first horse seemed to leap straight at us as it left the gate like a rocket, barely touching the ground. At the same time we ran for safety, finally hanging from our hands on a wooden fence. The animal threw its rider and did a circuit, coming perilously close to us. Princess Margaret and her party had leapt to their feet too, and, seeing the horse go by, smiled down on our obviously concerned faces. With relief we dropped to the ground, but the next animal did exactly the same thing, much to the amusement of the princess.

A little earlier the princess had left the royal train to board an old stagecoach for a ride in the arena with the governor. The horse team took off at speed, getting faster at every stride. When the driver realised they were getting out of control, outriders spurred their mounts on, racing alongside in real Western fashion, eventually bringing the horses to a halt. It was then a quiet ride into town.

Our coverage of Princess Margaret's overseas tours took us into areas with few facilities for producing rush pictures, which had to be taken to a radio station. Films and plates therefore had to be developed in pans, baking tins, tobacco tins, even cups – anything, in fact, that would hold liquid. In Arusha in East Africa, six photographers had to queue outside a hen-coop that had been converted for use as a darkroom – but it was far from light-proof.

A small single-engined plane waited on a rough clearing a mile or two away, to take the prints to Nairobi Radio Station. The first man to the plane had priority at the radio station to be the first to wire his print; the last man had to wait until the others were all cleared – about one and a half to two hours later. One man saw his pictures run away, having melted on the film base.

Although we were constantly flying around the world, we were always dressed for the part at each rendezvous, whether it was a garden party, service parade, reception or banquet. Clean shirts were our biggest problem and when we arrived at a new location for a night's stay, the rush was for the laundry. The local people often helped us by taking our dirty clothes down to the river and washing them there.

At the end of one long tour with Princess Margaret in the Caribbean, the press corps, which numbered about thirty, went to the

THE ROYAL ROSE

THE ROYAL ROSE

airport to photograph her leaving for London. Daily datelines and deadlines had been made, and sometimes missed through no fault of those with the pen or camera. A tour of six or nine weeks could bring sheer physical exhaustion and mental fatigue. As the aircraft left the ground a rush was made, as usual, for telephones and cables to give the last few words to a waiting press office in London. As each pressman replaced the receiver for the last time, his head was bowed for he knew that the chase was over and the tension had relaxed.

During Princess Margaret's East African tour, we were due to arrive one morning to photograph her on safari in the Serengeti National Park. When we arrived, there were in all about six local people to be seen, apart from the guards who were on duty at the hut where the princess had spent the night. An army officer barred our way at a distance of about two hundred yards from the perimeter of the hut, proclaiming that no pictures should be taken. Although we explained that we had been asked officially to cover the princess's trip, we were told adamantly that we should not photograph the building where she was staying, for security reasons, or to move forward. At a Government reception later that evening in Nairobi, the princess asked why we had not taken photographs that morning. We explained exactly what had happened and she accepted our explanation; after this incident, no such restriction happened again. The missed opportunity of photographing the princess in the Serengeti was a considerable loss to the newspapers, of course.

At one of the great gatherings of tribes at Mwanza from a wide area of East Africa, the men and women decked in every conceivable native dress were patiently waiting to get their drums on the beat and to move their dancing feet. Some delay occurred and the princess had vanished into a large marquee with a team of dignitaries. After what seemed a long time, a few pressmen went over to the drummers and learned how they made their instruments from hollowed-out tree trunks. There was also the added temptation of taking up the drumsticks, which were pieces of bone. Our interference started the drums beating and a few minutes later many vibrant drums echoed from all sides of the giant arena, the sound becoming louder as more teams joined the action. What we didn't know was that, once started, the infection of the drum beat to the tribesmen is hard to resist and each section tries to out-beat the other. It was some time before the beat could be stopped and the planned event could run.

On each of Princess Margaret's tours, the media increasingly speculated about her future husband. She met princes and socialites from all over the world, while the press took every opportunity of getting an intimate story or shot.

As Princess Margaret travelled around the world, the local media would conjure up romances that were linked with names of the members of their society. At state balls there was the constant question of who she would dance with and the ever-watchful eyes were ready for a sign that would indicate a love match. Columnists from the USA and Europe wrote pages of idle speculation, linking the princess with the most unlikely eligible bachelors.

Many pressmen lost a great deal of sleep in their efforts to report on the story of Peter Townsend's romance with Princess Margaret as they waited outside houses at Binfield and Uckfield for scraps of news. Foreign newsmen used wooden fences at Binfield to build fires along the road to keep them warm during the night.

Wherever ex-RAF Group Captain Peter Townsend arrived or departed from, or even when he was out riding, he met the media. He was always helpful and gave the times when he would leave his flat so that meantime we could take a much-needed break and have some food and warm drinks. When the talks at Uckfield finally ended and the romance between Princess Margaret and Peter Townsend was over, the long vigil of the media was over too.

After the wedding of Princess Margaret to Tony Armstrong-Jones, I watched the couple depart for their honeymoon in the royal yacht *Britannia* from a helicopter above them.

When the princess and her husband toured America, the press followed them to Hollywood, Tucson, New York and San Francisco. The superficial glamour and excitement of the trip glossed over the hard work of flying from one destination to another.

Over the years, I have travelled alongside and met both Princess Margaret and Lord Snowdon. They were always co-operative with the press and never hindered us in our work. It was particularly sad, therefore, to have to report the end of their marriage.

Some years later, I attended Kensington Registry Office to photograph the marriage of Lord Snowdon to Miss Lindsay Hogg.

THE ROYAL ROSE

6
BRITAIN'S BEST LOVED GRANNIE

The Queen Mother still fills the frames of our cameras with the same delight as she did in the 1920s – and that covers a great deal of photographic progress. Originally she was photographed with cameras with a fabric blind shutter that was opened or closed by means of a string loop to obtain the variable exposures. She has stood with patience as the photographer waited for the flash powder to ignite a blinding flame and has always been most courteous to the press.

The Queen Mother's early initiation into the world of press photographers began when she met a group of men who were limited in the equipment that was available. For everyday work, photographers seldom changed from a 5 x 4in or 9 x 12cm camera with plate or cut film, using a 5in lens with an aperture of f4.5. The fact that film was very slow in those early days caused technical problems that had to be overcome. If a photographer attempted to use a telephoto lens, he would have to focus first on a ground-glass screen. The depth of focus was so little on short distances, yet whether the Queen Mother was seven, five, four or even three yards from the cameras, she was always smiling.

During her trips to the London gardens of which she is so fond, the Queen Mother enjoys 'walkabouts', which allow her the opportunity to meet the general public. Intensely interested in everything around her, she is one of the most hard-working members of the royal family and the number of her engagements is remarkable for a lady of her age.

The centre of a family which is devoted to her, the Queen Mother has weathered the problems of her public and private life, particularly the problems among her own family.

When the romance between Peter Townsend and Princess Margaret became public knowledge, large numbers of journalists and photographers from all over the world camped outside Clarence

House and the Townsend home in Lowndes Square. The Queen Mother was at the centre of the talks concerning the family crisis that eventually led to the couple separating. Later, when the marriage of Lord Snowdon and Princess Margaret broke down, it was the Queen Mother who managed the situation with confidence.

When the Queen Mother visited the National Youth Orchestra, which was performing at the Royal Festival Hall in London, I photographed her, as usual, in one or two pre-arranged areas where she would stop. When I had finished taking the official photographs, the long line of young musicians were all anxious to talk to the royal personage. When I was about to leave, I received a message to return and take as many photographs of the Queen Mother and the young players as possible. The Queen Mother had noticed how eager the young musicians were to be photographed with her.

Always charmingly and immaculately dressed, it is the custom of the Queen Mother to wear hats that are off the face, so that she can be easily seen in public. When she is out of the public eye, however, she enjoys salmon fishing either at Deeside near Balmoral or in the waters near her home at the Castle of Mey, when she dresses in waders and waterproofs.

The Queen Mother's love of horse-racing is no secret and she enjoys to the full the progress of her stable of horses. She is often seen at Newbury, Newmarket, Epsom, and of course at Ascot during the summer. Jockeys, trainers, stewards, horse owners, the head lads and even those retired from the horse-racing world are her friends. The Queen Mother's long experience in the world of horse-racing has made her known as an authority on the sport.

On one of her birthdays, I was among a number of photographers who had gathered outside her home to see her. When she did not appear the media lost patience and went away. After Princess Margaret with her two children had arrived carrying birthday gifts, the doors closed behind them. The crowd swelled to a few hundred, and the guards band marched past, playing 'Happy Birthday', on their way to the changing of the guard ceremony at Buckingham Palace. Voices from the crowd joined in the song and, as the music faded into the distance, the crowd continued singing. Then the large gates of the drive slowly opened and the Queen Mother appeared carrying a posy of flowers and wearing a radiant smile. She came towards the crowd as close as possible and thanked the well-wishers profusely. Since then, whenever she is in London on her birthday, a rousing chorus of 'Happy Birthday' echoes across The Mall to celebrate her popularity.

BRITAIN'S
BEST LOVED GRANNIE

7
UNFORGETTABLE OCCASIONS

Everyone experiences bad days, when they are relieved to climb into bed and forget the world. One such unforgettable experience occurred during the royal tour of the Queen and Prince Philip to New Zealand in 1963. We had been rushing to cover all the events and when things calmed down, the late Vincent Mulchrone of the *Daily Mail* and I went into a bar at Russell for a much needed drink. We had to battle to the counter to get a schooner and a jug of beer from the bar, after which we rushed on to our next venue.

The next stop was in Auckland where, after a hectic morning of engagements and a regatta, our venue was a party for press representatives given by the Queen on board the royal yacht *Britannia*. While she was talking to members of the local media, Vincent and I were quietly standing in one corner of the famous quarter-deck, taking a small glass of whisky and water, while recalling our experience of buying a drink in Russell. Vincent, whose Irish Yorkshire humour was a constant source of amusement on tour, reminisced about our days on speeding boats, planes and trains, the memories of which made us both laugh. At this point, we were ushered towards the Queen who enquired about the source of our amusement. I explained that Vincent was embellishing the story of how we bought a drink in Russell. In his own inimitable way, he recalled how deep in bodies it was to the bar and how a small lip on the edge stopped the beer from spilling over. He explained how we had waited to get a couple of schooners as they floated by, then waited again when a jug was passed down, which had to be grabbed and pulled through the bodies to fill the glasses. By this time we were all laughing, but I was suddenly aware that I was unable to hold my slippery glass and, as my grip loosened, the glass slipped through my fingers and crashed beside the Queen's feet.

It was as if somebody had fired a shot. Suddenly, all conversation had ceased and the whole assembly was shocked into silence. All eyes were riveted on my face. At that moment I would have been happy if the deck had opened and swallowed me up. My face went red and my hands broke into a sweat. Offering my profuse apologies to the Queen, she stepped aside from the broken glass and asked what happened next at Russell.

Voices slowly began to rise, the glass fragments were cleared, my drink was replaced and the story continued. It was indeed one of the most embarrassing moments of my life.

Shortly after leaving the ship, I read in the local newspaper of 'The Queen's narrow escape'. I was the subject of news which was hardly wanted. I was also in a hurry because I was covering the official visit of the Queen to St James Theatre. In my evening attire, standing about ten feet away from the chosen exit door of the royal party and the premier as they departed, my flash failed. I tried to adjust it by pushing in the electric leads, but again it failed. While I was still trying to make the flash work, the Queen leaned over and quietly said to me 'It's not your day today, Mr Reed, is it?' At that moment I could have hugged her and the tension of the moment was totally relaxed. The outcome of my press coverage was just one picture. As the procession reached the cars the Queen's final words to me, which were said with a broad smile on her face, were 'It's just not your day, Mr Reed!'

The story of the broken glass grew in the dailies and magazines to such an extent that by the time we reached Napier, the tale of the disgusting drunken pressman who had tipped a drink down the Queen's dress, was being discussed in the mayoral parlour, within my hearing.

The story has been retold around the world. Not only am I supposed to have done the deed in Auckland, but also in Christchurch, Wellington, Perth, Sydney, Adelaide, and in many other ports. The contents of my glass is always a gin and tonic, but occasionally the story is retold that the Queen's stockings and dress were damaged by the incident. There is no doubt that the story is embellished each time it is retold.

During a royal tour of Southeast Asia, during which we had visited Singapore, Malaya, Borneo and Thailand on a day-to-day programme, I was ambling down to the quay to await the arrival of the Queen. A sudden pain in the chest momentarily made me stop, but it eased and I carried on. Later that evening I was examined by the Queen's doctor and before the night was out, I was already in hospital suffering a heart-attack.

The royal tour continued on its way and I received good-will messages from the Queen who was sent a daily progress report on my recovery. It was particularly cheering to receive a message from the Queen that if I was not able to travel by air, then *Britannia* was at my disposal.

One of the most memorable occasions of my life was when I received the Order of the British Empire at Buckingham Palace in 1978. As the Queen pinned the medal on my lapel, she put me totally at ease when she said, 'This is for all your battle scars on royal tours.'

THE
PHOTOGRAPHS

This picture has always given me pleasure. The family stands waiting at their front door in Paisley, Scotland, while the father bows deeply in courtesy to the Queen – a delightful touch depicting a family's regard for Her Majesty.

(Opposite): *The Queen loves Scotland and always looks happy when she arrives there. This was taken outside Paisley Station in 1953 at the beginning of her Scottish tour soon after her coronation. The Queen always looked relaxed during this tour.*

(Left): *The pictures which capture the heart of royal family life are these two of the late Lord Louis Mountbatten and his wife Lady Edwina helping Prince Charles and Princess Anne do a little paddling. These rare shots brought a stream of delighted letters from families across the country. On this occasion, the two children were in Malta in 1954, about to join the Queen and Prince Philip making a state visit.*

(Above): *Wherever the Queen went during her tour of Malta in 1954 a huge battery of cameras were recording every movement. Here she was about to board a ship to visit the island of Gozo.*

Looking exceedingly neat, the tiny figure of Prince Charles is dwarfed by officers of the armed forces as he steps ashore in Valletta, Malta, to see the Queen attending a reception. The occasion was a visit by the Queen and Prince Philip to the island in 1954 during their royal tour. Princess Anne was also in the party.

(Opposite): *On the quayside at Valletta, Malta, in 1954: Prince Charles goes on an outing with his favourite uncle, Lord Louis Mountbatten. This photograph is one of Prince Charles's most treasured and has a prominent place in his collection.*

It was early in the morning that the Queen's plane touched down in North Africa to visit the graves of the men and women who died during World War II. For the Queen and Prince Philip, it was a moving experience.

We were using large cameras needing either glass plates or cut film, and a plane was waiting on the tarmac to carry the images to London. Just as the royal plane touched down, David McNeil of the Sunday Pictorial *discovered his shutter had jammed. As he opened his Rolleiflex camera, the front fell out. He banged his large camera on the ground in desperation and the shutter unjammed itself just in time to take his photographs.*

46

(Opposite): *On the early tours of Princess Margaret, such as this one in 1955 to the West Indies, our cameras were not capable of quickly changing to a wide angle lens. As every gown the princess wore was magnificent, it was vital that each picture was full length. Often the cameramen were crowded at the foot of the stairs against a wall to make this possible. David Johnson of* the Daily Sketch *and I decided that we would solve the problem with the co-operation of the princess. I would collect a bloom from the garden and place it on a selected stair where the princess would stop, so that we could get pictures like this one. Occasionally the princess would tease us by stepping over the flower, but then she would laugh and go back and pose for us.*

The window frames of the Denbigh Agriculture Training College was a good spot in Kingston, Jamaica, to see Princess Margaret close up.

(Left): *We had waited some time for Princess Margaret to pass that way in Jamaica on her way to the royal yacht. To keep the calypso band happy we made sure that they had plenty to drink and the result was this delightful picture under the palms.*

(Above). From whatever part of the world, children are always eye-catching, not only because of their dress, but because they are uninhibited. A good child or animal picture such as this one taken in the West Indies in 1955, which shows a child yawning repeatedly as she waited for the arrival of Princess Margaret, always brings lots of letters to the paper concerned.

(Right): *Princess Margaret and Lord Snowdon on a cable car in San Francisco during the rush hour. They were travelling from Fisherman's Wharf to Powell during their visit to the United States in 1956.*

(Opposite): *Looking extremely cool, the Queen arrives at a ceremony to welcome her to Lagos, Nigeria, in 1956. She was to tour the country and attend one of the greatest gathering of tribesmen and women ever seen. They came on foot, on horse and by camel from hundreds of miles to the town of Kaduna, their belongings being carried for them by a retinue of followers. Dressed in splendid robes, and stirrups made of gold encrusted with jewels, bearing swords in golden scabbards and parading to ceaseless music and the beat of drums, they started at first light. The Queen wore a splendid gown and diamond tiara, and sat from eight o'clock until noon, in the heat of the sun, to see them pass. As a finale, numerous horsemen galloped past the Queen in a cloud of dust.*

(Left): *With arms folded, this royal
enthusiast in Mombasa had been
waiting patiently for many hours to
catch a glimpse of Princess Margaret
during her tour of East Africa in 1956.*

(Above): *During the Queen's visit to
Lagos, this young lady stepped forward
and presented her with a bouquet. It
was a magic moment, one that for me
makes taking photographs a delight.*

(Left): *The dancer's special shoes that made the sound of drums as he danced accompanied by his own music really made him a star at Mwanza, East Africa, where Princess Margaret toured in 1956.*

(Above): *During Princess Margaret's visit to East Africa in 1956 baby John was put into a bath just as she arrived to look around the mothercraft class. Being in the right place at the right moment to capture such a delightful scene is the reason why photographers on a royal tour must keep up with events all the time.*

Taken in the morning of an October day in 1956 at Arusha in East Africa, Princess Margaret was very pleased to feed a friendly giraffe at an animal farm. This was one of the quieter moments of her tour, away from the huge crowd that gathered every time she appeared.

Photographers had to produce prints for the radio based in Nairobi. Six competing staffers from the London dailies were given a hen-coop for the purpose. It was made of weather-boarding containing an enlarger where after only a few minutes inside, out of tropical sunshine, people could see each other. I was bent almost double using a tobacco tin as a developing tank. Others used anything that held liquid. The heat allowed only $1\frac{1}{2}$ minutes developing time, then the film went into the hypo and the first photographer to finish was able to use the enlarger. I had earlier made a wet printing frame for such moments. One or two lost their shots as the emulsion melted from the film base in the heat.

Wet prints in hand, we all rushed to a waiting aircraft, the pilot timing each in turn, and then straight to the radio station. The photographs were wired to London on a first come first served basis – the last often had to wait as long as an hour or more.

(Left): *This young boy's mother had already been praised for her beauty and she has obviously spent a great deal of time and trouble to make herself look perfect for a huge gathering of tribes in East Africa to greet Princess Margaret. But the excitement, the drums and the dancing were too much for the young lad, and the smart little robe he was wearing was a hindrance. This striking shot is a treasured moment, when just one delightful picture can make the whole journey worthwhile.*

War canoes roar down-river to greet the Queen at Port Harcourt, Nigeria. The canoes were propelled only by the strength of the enthusiastic paddlers who put every effort into gaining speed. A tribal chief sits on his throne in the bow with his attendants. The boat looked overloaded, but the Africans always turned out in numbers on royal occasions. It was not possible to discover who was giving the orders above the sound of the drums.

The Swedish royal barge ties up at the landing. The Queen and Prince Philip step ashore to be greeted by the King of Sweden, with his queen a few paces behind. In the June sunshine, with the streets lined with people, sights such as this are always the highlight of royal tours.

(Opposite): While she was paying an official visit to Sweden in June 1956 the Queen paid an informal visit to an ordinary home during her tour of Stockholm. She went through the garden gate and into the kitchen where she sat down with the family.

(Above): *A tribal gathering in Mwanza, East Africa, during Princess Margaret's tour in 1956. I always shoot as much film as possible on these occasions.*

(Right): *Mother of Princess Alexandra, Princess Marina is shielded from the tropical sun in Accra, Ghana, during her tour of the country.*

60

(Above): *King Frederick of Denmark and the Queen were old friends and enjoyed a good relationship. When she arrived in Copenhagen in 1957 it was cool, so the king ordered her fur to be brought and wouldn't let the procession proceed until she was comfortable.*

(Right): *When the Lieutenant Governor of British Honduras walked with Princess Margaret along the street in Belize, he had the problem of avoiding her parasol because of his tall headpiece. The princess was visiting this country after her tour of the West Indies in 1958.*

The photograph of this Trinidadian girl who was waiting at the roadside to meet Princess Margaret was published in magazines worldwide. The princess was visiting Port of Spain, Trinidad, in 1958 and the carnival was about to start. The girl's companion simply had to take a closer look at her when my camera was aimed at her face. Her large soft eyes captured my heart and I captured her image on film to delight the eyes of readers everywhere.

(Left): *After a long flight to Heathrow to end a lengthy tour of the Commonwealth, the Queen Mother stepped sprightly towards the airport building. She looked as if she had just left home after a long rest. As usual, she was brimming with life and walked with a spring in her step.*

The royal standard is tied to the cowboy driver's seat and Princess Margaret looks out of the antique stagecoach at a Canadian Mountie moving the steps. She was on her way to a rodeo at Williams Lake, British Columbia, in 1958. The team of horses went full gallop, the outriders chased after them and eventually brought them in check. The princess's escort climbed down to remove a fly that was biting a tender part of the lead horse's body. Afterwards, she enjoyed a pleasant ride into town.

Dressed for the part in rubber boots, a heavy macintosh and a hood, Princess Margaret gets a soaking as she heads for Niagara Falls in the tunnel. There was no doubt that it was a very wet occasion.

(Opposite): *Using a Hasselblad with a 250mm lens I took a close-up shot of Princess Margaret when she was attending a garden party during a royal tour of Canada in 1958. She had then earned the title of Fairy Tale Princess and looked radiant at every stage of her journey.*

(Above): *There are rare occasions when an ordinary event turns into an extraordinary one such as occurred in La Fontaine Park, Montreal, when Princess Margaret was signing the visitor's book. As we came upon the scene she was handed a pen and wrote her name in large letters. It was the largest VIP. register I had ever seen.*

The Queen walks alone on the deck of
Britannia *during the opening ceremony
of the St Lawrence Seaway in June
1959. Her Majesty is rarely seen
alone. On this occasion she was
accompanied by a party of Canadian
and American visitors, including
President Eisenhower, Prime Minister
Diefenbaker and their wives. As the
yacht entered the locks, strings
attached to large tapes were broken and
set off explosions and music. The after-
deck of* Britannia *looked deserted.*

(Opposite): *Even the Canadian
Mountie with his strong arm didn't
stop this little fellow photographing the
Queen as she drove by in her car.*

*Everybody, everywhere wants to
photograph the Queen when she is on
tour. She is probably the most
photographed woman in the world and
millions of films have been used to
capture her image. She has caused a
rush on films and developing in many
towns and cities around the world. I
myself have spent many long days
following her on tour, often starting at
dawn and finishing in the early hours
of the following morning.*

(Left): *When the Queen stepped from the royal train at Stratford, Ontario, on her way to attend the Shakespeare Theatre, the press had to run along the track to get this picture, follow the entourage round the town, then run to catch the train again. Unfortunately, we had to run alongside the train to catch up with our carriages that were some way down the track and already moving. As soon as the Queen stepped onto the train it began to move and we even had to run through people's gardens to catch up. I was thankful for a helping hand from the Queen's lady-in-waiting, Lady Dorothy Egerton, as I leapt onto the train.*

(Above): *Even in a crowded street where thousands of people line the pavement edges, the Queen is extremely observant. As she travelled in her car through Arvida, Canada, in 1959, she recognised an acquaintance and acknowledged them. Her specially made car with a plastic back was a great success as she could be seen whatever the weather.*

71

*The Prince of Wales is being
introduced to the people by Her Majesty
the Queen at Caernarvon Castle in
1969.*

In 1960 Princess Anne was a
bridesmaid at the wedding of Lady
Pamela Mountbatten and Mr. David
Hicks at Romsey Abbey. At a party at
the village hall estate workers and
villagers joined in the celebrations.
Here, Princess Anne and Prince
Charles watch intently as the bride and
groom cut the cake – a replica of
Broadlands, the home of the late Lord
and Lady Mountbatten.

The last photograph taken at the
wedding of Lady Pamela Mountbatten
and Mr David Hicks. It snowed and
rained, but everybody had a thoroughly
enjoyable day. Princess Anne was all
smiles on the way to the reception in a
car with rain-splashed windows.

(Left): *During a tour of Nigeria in 1960, Princess Alexandra danced with her equerry, Captain George Kurobo. Wherever she went, the princess captured the hearts of all she met.*

(Above): *During a tour of West Africa in 1961, the royal couple had been watching a youth display and virgin dances in Freetown. Prince Philip, who usually takes his own pictures on such occasions, is carrying a mini camera. The Queen is wearing full evening dress, even though it is lunchtime and tremendously hot. If she thinks that the people would prefer to see her in a full length gown she obliges, despite the heat or time of day. Something has attracted her attention during the proceedings and she makes a quiet remark to her husband on the royal dais. Sitting immediately behind her is a young Scout.*

The Queen is delighted to receive a present from this little girl at Sierra Leone in 1961. The girl's mother had spent a great deal of time stitching a dress with pictures of the Queen printed in the material.

(Opposite): *The Queen was on a tour of Ghana in 1961 and on display in a departmental store in Accra was a collection of replicas of the crown jewels. I was delighted to capture the smiling face of the young boy about to be 'crowned' by his friends.*

(Above): *The Queen's pathway was strewn with flower petals in Ghana during her visit in 1961. Wherever she went she received a rapturous welcome and the market mammies greeted her with a huge poster that read 'Lizzie smile on us again'. They sang to her at every step of her way. Their enthusiasm and happiness was infectious and the drums had a wonderful beat.*

(Left): *The author is explaining the workings of a camera to topless girls in West Africa in 1961.*

(Above): *The Queen and Prince Philip in the royal gondola on the Grand Canal in Venice on their way to watch a gala on the water. It is a difficult shot to execute with confidence because aiming in the dark at an unlit subject on water makes it difficult to judge the distance. Consequently, pictures such as this are not very sharp in definition.*

(Right): *A rare picture showing the Queen's meeting with the Pope in Rome in 1961. The Queen's stunning gown was set off with a diamond tiara and pearl necklace. Her escort is a Swiss Guard. It is a rare privilege for English photographers to be allowed to take photographs inside the Vatican.*

(Left): *When the Queen and Prince Philip were touring Holland in 1962, they were received by Queen Juliana and Prince Bernhardt in the Throne Room of the Dam Palace in Amsterdam. I was positioned behind* *the plants in the fireplace, from where I suddenly appeared when the Queen reached that spot. After taking a quick photograph, I hid once again behind the plants, much to the Queen's amusement.*

(Above): *Princess Beatrix, now Queen of the Netherlands, and alongside her (in naval uniform) Prince Bernhardt, husband of Queen Juliana, accompanying the Queen during her tour of Holland.*

The Queen joins the children on a walk-about in Sydney, Australia, in 1963. The children could hardly believe that they could walk down the road with the Queen on her tour of their country.

Wearing steel helmets to protect them from possible injury, the Queen and Prince Philip take off in a truck which carried them under the mountains at the Geehi Dam in Australia. They were visiting the hydro-electric scheme in the Snowy Mountains. Their tour took them not only around the coast and the big cities, but to Catherine, Alice Springs and down the west coast.

Thousands of schoolchildren, men and women thronged the stadium in Brisbane, Australia, and hemmed the royal couple's Land-Rover into a tight situation. To the four corners of the ground, there were excited people. This scene in 1963 made an exceptional picture and proved the popularity of the royal pair.

There's no way of controlling the wind in Wellington when it decides to get up, even though the hems of the Queen's dresses are weighted. The wayward wind gave the Queen a tricky moment or two as she stepped from her car at Wellington, New Zealand, in 1963 on her way to a new estate at Porirua. At first, she tried to hold down the hem of her dress. Then, with a smile, she gave in gracefully and walked away showing a little more knee than her dressmaker intended. Prince Philip chose to ignore the incident, for there is nothing any escort, however gallant, can do in a situation like this.

An exciting moment for the huge crowd waiting patiently for a glimpse of the Queen in New Zealand in 1963. They were treated to a rare sight as she walked with Prime Minister Holyoak. She was wearing a beautiful gown and sparkling tiara.

King Constantine of the Hellenes with his bride Princess Anne-Marie of Denmark riding through the streets of Athens after their wedding at Athens Cathedral in 1964. The marriage was attended by many members of the royal families from all over the world, including Prince Charles and *Princess Anne, who found time to visit the Parthenon.*

By pre-arrangement, I had a taxi driver standing by to take me to the airport to catch a London-bound plane with only a few minutes to spare. I was then back home in time for the following day's edition.

Prince Philip was called El Duque when he toured Mexico in 1964. He looked the part, too, sporting his six guns and wearing the right outfit, including a sombrero as he headed for the stables at the ranch of the late Merle Oberon, the film star. A few minutes later he was in a cloud of dust riding among the cactus plants.

(Left): *Princess Margaret and Lord Snowdon find some peace during a busy American tour in 1965. Here they are relaxing in the sun on a farm at Tucson, having called on the owner, Mr Lewis Douglas, a former US ambassador to Britain.*

(Opposite): *The top picture of a young girl trying to reach forward to kiss Prince Philip when he was visiting Mexico in 1964 became a royal picture of the year. However alert, security men sometimes cannot prevent such intimacies from happening. For this reason photographers must keep up with members of the royal family when they are on tour. Prince Philip's relaxed manner assured him of a friendly reception. When this señorita tried to give him a kiss, a local newspaper enthused: 'The duke's popularity mounts as more Mexicans see him.' The señorita failed to give him a kiss, and was held back by security guards, but she did receive a pat on the cheek from Prince Philip.* (see opposite below).

(Above): *It was a hot and very dusty climb to reach the 9,000ft point above sea level, but the Queen with Emperor Haile Selassie never hesitated. They reached the top to view the famous Tississat Falls, on the Nile, in Ethiopia, where the Queen was on tour in 1965. Photographers loaded down with their equipment found it hard to keep up.*

(Right): *When she was presented with a skin drum during her tour of Uganda in 1965, Princess Margaret couldn't resist the temptation to tap out a beat with her fingers. Even though she was on a platform in front of a huge crowd, had made a speech and signed the visitor's book, that human touch was appreciated by everyone.*

Princess Margaret gave this creature the name 'Shuffleoff' when she met one of the animals on the farm at Micheson Falls, Uganda, during her tour in 1965. She was demonstrating the fact that it had no horns, but she appeared to be doing a bull-ring dance.

At the Museum of Modern Art, New York, Princess Margaret appears to be fetching the water, and the figure, a statue called 'Girl' by Reg Butler, disrobing. Utilising the situation of the fountains made this photograph come alive, but it was only published as a small picture.

(Opposite): A helmet on top of a headscarf may not be elegant, but it was a necessary protection when the Queen visited a steelworks at Duisburg in the heart of West Germany's industrial region. The Queen and Prince Philip made a long tour of West Germany in 1965 where they received a warm welcome.

The Queen with members of the family enjoy an outing in the grounds of Frogmore, Windsor, with Prince Andrew giving a helping hand with Prince Edward's pram. When the pram halted, the five-year-old Prince Andrew put on the brake to stop it from moving forward, while Princess Anne helped Prince Edward to keep his head above the pillows. Prince Andrew then played among the daffodils climbing the banks and picking a flower for his mother as they passed the lake. Princess Anne placed a daffodil on Prince Edward's head, which made the Queen smile. It was a happy family gathering. I had been asked to take photographs to celebrate the Queen's thirty-ninth birthday on 21 April 1965, and the pictures were used worldwide.

98

This was a moment in history for two nations. It was also a moment that John Kennedy's son will treasure all his life. The four-year-old shakes hands with the Queen so shyly, but so proudly too. Master John Kennedy with his mother Jacqueline and sister, Caroline with Richard and Edward Kennedy visited Runnymede beside the Thames for the unveiling of the President John Kennedy memorial by the Queen in May 1965.

Princess Anne and Prince Charles take a ride on a raft down the Rio Grande in Jamaica during their tour of the West Indies.

(Right): *Uncrowned soccer King Pele meets the Queen after winning in a friendly match between Rio and São Paulo (Pele captained the latter) in the Maracana Stadium. The Queen laughed and talked to Pele, telling him to hold the cup higher.*

In line to meet King Olaf from the royal barge at Trondheim, the Queen takes the children for an afternoon out. When the children were small, they rarely stepped out of line. If they did, a glance from their mother soon corrected them.

102

The Queen and Prince Philip left an Eskimo dwelling at one o'clock in the morning. It was still light in the land of the midnight sun, at a spot named Tuktoyaktuk on the Beaufort Sea. Although it was summer, everyone was wearing thick coats, except the press as we had been told incorrectly that the temperature would not drop below 50°F. We all shivered in our inadequate clothing, but the Queen, who was wearing knee-length boots, looked warm. It was a surprise to us when we went to bed after midnight, as all the children were still playing outside.

103

(Above): *The Queen suppresses a smile as Prince Philip peeps from behind an official while they were watching an army display at Shilo in the North West Territories of Canada during their 1970 tour.*

(Right): *It rained, then snowed, at Tuktoyaktuk in the Arctic as the Queen, Prince Charles and Princess Anne arrived to view the midnight sun. They were suitably clad in parkas, but their wait was in vain. Unfortunately, there was nothing to see in the sky but cloud.*

(Opposite): *It was all excitement when Prince Charles presented this young lady with the Beauty Queen prize during his tour of Canada. The prince has a keen eye for a pretty girl, but it was a surprise when the young beauty stuck out her tongue when he announced the winner. The Indian in the background obviously thought she looked good too.*

(Above): *As the two giant helicopters neared the stands they caused a gale. The Queen simply had to hang on to her hat, while the army officer half closed his eyes and said nothing. The incident took place at Shilo, Canada, when the Queen with Prince Philip, Prince Charles and Princess Anne toured the North West Territories in 1970.*

(Right): *This portrait of Prince Charles and Princess Anne was acclaimed as the best royal picture of 1970. Taken in the Arctic, the royal pair had just begun their tour of Canada's North West Territories and the Eskimos had given them warm, windproof parkas. It was a freezing cold day and they were enjoying a great deal of laughter.*

When Princess Anne presented

the photographic awards at London's Royal Lancaster Hotel, she said: 'If I may pick out one of the winners, a familiar face to me is Freddie Reed, who has been taking royal pictures for longer than I can remember. He has been around professionally twice as long as I have.' This picture was rejected when it arrived in London. It was used later as a birthday picture and only then was it praised.

During the royal family's tour of Canada in 1970, Prince Charles enjoys the midnight beach party at Yellowknife.

(Opposite): *Princess Anne in serious conversation with some of the two thousand guests, at a giant beach party at McNiven beach in Canada's North West Territories. A young child in the background listens intently.*

109

During a trip to East Africa, Princess Anne appeared with a 35mm camera ready to compete with the photographers around her. She had been visiting children on behalf of the Save the Children Fund and was about to enjoy a day off-duty.

Princess Anne is an expert amateur photographer. She can often be seen working from the shadows using long focus equipment, and even takes straight eye-to-eye shots of cameramen. At every opportunity, members of the royal family use cameras, the Queen being the most enthusiastic. Prince Charles is the only member of the royal family who has yet to be seen with a camera in his hands.

(Opposite top): *Treetops, Kenya, where the Queen heard the news that her father, George VI, had died. It was a quiet moment for Princess Anne while she read the giant plaque situated in the Mgumu tree that reads: 'In the Mgumu tree Her Royal Highness Princess Elizabeth and his Royal Highness the Duke of Edinburgh, spent the night of February 5, 1952. While here Princess Elizabeth succeeded to the throne through the death of her father King George the Sixth.'*

A moment in our history happened here in the heart of Kenya and Princess Anne was obviously moved by visiting the famous Sangana Lodge, where her mother and father received the news of the king's death. From there the Queen and Prince Philip returned to England, curtailing their tour.

(Opposite): *In the heat of the midday sun outside Nairobi, Kenya, Princess Anne joins the children of a local school. She was on a tour in connection with the Save the Children Fund and was accompanied by Valerie Singleton of the BBC.*

TREETOPS KENYA

IN THIS MGUMU TREE

AT A POINT HIGHER THE PRINCESS ELIZABETH

AND

HER ROYAL HIGHNESS THE DUKE OF EDINBURGH

VISIT OF FEBRUARY 5th 1952

WHEN PRINCESS ELIZABETH

ACCEDED TO THE THRONE THROUGH

THE DEATH OF HER FATHER

KING GEORGE THE SIXTH

THE REMAINS OF THE
ORIGINAL TREETOPS CAN
BE SEEN ON THE OTHER
SIDE OF THE WATERHOLE

(Left): *Prince Charles sports a four-day growth of beard arriving back at a spot 50 miles in the bush outside Isiolo, Kenya, after a camel safari. He was surrounded by armed guards and other members of his party. Our journeys back and forth to Nairobi by car were often very long, for we had also to attend the engagements of Princess Anne who was based in the capital.*

(Above): *It was not a luxurious journey for Prince Charles who led a camel train into the wild 20 miles outside Isiolo, Kenya, in 1971. He went on safari into isolated country and lived under canvas. We arranged to meet him at this spot after a bumpy, dusty ride in a Land-Rover. There landscape was nothing but bush, but the head game-warden Dennis*

Zaphiro, who carried a gun, was an expert guide. A few days later we met again near the same spot. The prince was wearing a small beard, while we had travelled several hundred miles on our chartered plane from Nairobi and on the Land-Rover. The working days were long, but the Stanley Hotel in Nairobi was always a welcoming sight.

(Above): *A very proud Prince Philip stands on the steps of RAF Cranwell after his son Prince Charles has been presented with his wings during a passing-out parade ceremony in August 1971.*

(Right): *It was supposed to be a secret and the Ministry of Defence refused to tell the picture and news editors the date and location of Prince Charles's first parachute jump in 1971. There was a total stop on information. I was advised by a contact to visit Studland Bay in Dorset, as the jumps are normally done over water. I was astonished, therefore, to find all the car parks filled on a week day in July. A car park attendant gave me all the information I needed: 'Don't watch the*

first aircraft, wait for the second, forget the first man out, the second is Prince Charles.'

Putting a doubler on my 1,000mm lens and taking just one shot as the parachute headed for the sea, I achieved this shot that made the front page. It proves that the photographer must not fail at the first obstacle. The photograph was taken on a Nikon operating at 2,000mm, 500th second at about f8.

(Above): *Two queens raise their glasses in a toast, at a state banquet in Bangkok, Thailand. This was the end of a day of great activity during a long tour of Southeast Asia in 1972. Both Queen Sirikit and the Queen thought this a very pleasant moment. It is a rare picture, for the Queen seldom drinks in public.*

(Right): *The bond of friendship is tied in a royal palace in Chiang Mai, Thailand, where King Bumphipol and Queen Sirikit joined the Queen, Prince Philip and Princess Anne for the ceremony. Later they saw hundreds of young girls, each carrying a lantern, dancing in the dark. We had dined early and were served by beautiful Thai girls.*

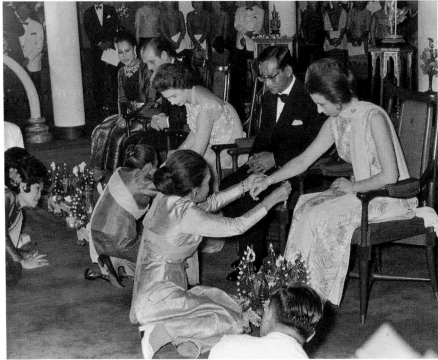

The royal family Orders were first given to the royal ladies by George IV in 1820. The Queen wears two of them – those of her father and grandfather. They are hand-painted miniatures on ivory, set in diamonds.

During a visit to Malaysia in 1972 Prince Philip won the affection of a new admirer, a lively young redhead called Aminah. She flung her arms around him and cuddled him shamelessly. Aminah, with her gorgeous hair of burnished copper, is an orang-utan from a breeding centre that was opened by the prince in Kuala Lumpur. The World Wildlife Fund, of which Prince Philip is a trustee, helped to build the centre in a bid to save the orang-utan from extinction. The prince was slightly less enthusiastic about Aminah's affection. When he put her down he said 'She weighs a ton.'

(Opposite): *Prince Charles arrives on the sun-drenched island of St Kitts in the Caribbean where he took part in the independence ceremony in 1973. He enjoyed a walkabout and talked to both the local boys and girls. Some of them were bashful, but others replied cheerfully. On this occasion he was opening the restored Prince of Wales Bastion, the island's fortress landmark. As I was on holiday in Barbados, I was obviously the most readily available photographer. After taking these pictures, it was a quick flight back to the beach.*

(Left): *Even though it was a little cold, Princess Anne and her bridegroom Captain Mark Phillips set off down Buckingham Palace Road in an open landau on the way to their honeymoon. All the pomp and ceremony over, they were at last on their own. Crowds lined the route to wave them off.*

(Above): *Princess Anne looked delightful in her large hat, but the face in the window made an ordinary photograph into a good picture. The delighted face at the window was* astonished at being so close to the princess when she opened a centre for young people at the National Maritime Museum in Greenwich.

(Above): *The Queen received a tumultuous welcome wherever she went during her Silver Jubilee celebrations. Flowers were handed to her from all sides, but it seems that nearly everybody could boast that they had touched the Queen. The Queen obviously loved it all and deserved the welcome.*

122

(Right): *During the Queen's Silver Jubilee celebrations, everybody from near and far joined in. The Queen went on long walkabouts and chatted to men, women and children in the streets. They obviously loved her for it.*

(Above): *Retiring from the staff of the* Daily Mirror *after fifty-one years took me into the BBC television studio for a live interview. An urgent request to try to get a picture of the Queen Mother leaving for her holidays while I was on my way back to Fleet Street made me rush for a taxi. Albert Foster, a colleague, joined me at Clarence House. To my astonishment, I was ushered into the house to meet the Queen Mother herself. 'I hear you are leaving today,' she said to me. 'You've* travelled so many miles with us. We'll miss you. You have helped us a great deal.' I replied: 'Oh no, Your Majesty, you have always helped us, and on behalf of all Fleet Street photographers I want to thank you.' We chatted and then I asked if it would be possible to take her portrait and she obliged happily. She knows that I like soft light, not sunlight, for portraits and her car was moved away to let me take this picture.*

(Right): *Prince Charles has always been fond of the Queen Mother and is extremely proud of her, not only for her friendship, but also her wisdom.*

*Dash, the eighteen-month-old pet of the
Queen Mother, peeping from behind
the Duchess of York and the Queen
when they joined the Queen Mother for
her birthday in 1988.*

INDEX